DATE DUE

MAY 0 6 2011			

FOLLETT

21st
Century
Skills Library

COOL CAREERS

TEACHER

Kevin Cunningham

Cherry Lake Publishing
Ann Arbor, Michigan

Published in the United States of America by Cherry Lake Publishing
Ann Arbor, Michigan
www.cherrylakepublishing.com

Content Adviser: Ward Weldon, PhD, Professor, College of Education, University of
Illinois at Chicago

Photo Credits: Cover and page 1, ©Rob Marmion, used under license from Shutterstock,
Inc.; page 4, ©Tatiana Mironenko, used under license from Shutterstock, Inc.; page 6,
©The Print Collector/Alamy; page 8, ©The MacLean Collection/Alamy; page 12, ©Stock
Connection Blue/Alamy; page 14, ©Tetra Images/Alamy;
page 17, ©iStockphoto.com/track5; page 18, ©JUPITERIMAGES/Brand X/Alamy; page
21, ©iStockphoto.com/lisapics; page 22, ©moodboard/Alamy; page 25, ©visage media
services pvt ltd/Alamy

Library of Congress Cataloging-in-Publication Data
Cunningham, Kevin.
Teacher / by Kevin Cunningham.
    p. cm.—(Cool careers)
Includes index.
ISBN-13: 978-1-60279-298-2
ISBN-10: 1-60279-298-4
1. Teachers—Vocational guidance—United States—Juvenile literature
I. Title. II. Series.
LB1775.2.C86 2009
317.10023—dc22   2008010475

---

*Cherry Lake Publishing would like to acknowledge the work of
The Partnership for 21st Century Skills.
Please visit www.21stcenturyskills.org for more information.*

TABLE OF CONTENTS

CHAPTER ONE
The History of Teaching   4

CHAPTER TWO
On the Job   12

CHAPTER THREE
From Student to Teacher   18

CHAPTER FOUR
The Future of Teaching   25

Some Famous Teachers   29

Glossary   30

For More Information   31

Index   32

About the Author   32

THE HISTORY OF TEACHING

Sometimes teachers come to school early or stay late to help students.

The final bell surprised Shari. She had not even noticed her classmates packing up. She was too absorbed in her social studies book. Since she always walked home from school, there was no need to hurry. And she really wanted to talk to Ms. Thatcher about the map of Ireland in her book. She went up to her teacher's desk.

"There's something I don't get about the homework," Shari said. "Except I don't want to make you stay late."

Ms. Thatcher laughed. "I stay late all the time. The kids get to go home when the bell rings, but the teachers always have work to do."

"Like homework?" Shari asked, confused.

"It's kind of like homework. Tonight, I'll take home the class's tests to grade. And your progress notes are due in a few days, so I want to finish them on time."

"Why do you have to do work at home?" Shari asked.

"Because I teach all day," Ms. Thatcher said.

As Shari lifted her book onto the desk, she said, "This one map is confusing."

"Turn to the page," Ms. Thatcher said. "I'll be happy to explain."

Aristotle taught Alexander the Great.

"It really won't make you late?"

"Believe it or not," Ms. Thatcher answered, "teachers like to hear students ask questions. Even after the bell."

Teachers have always played a role in human learning. In prehistoric societies, older family and tribe members passed along skills—hunting, farming, and toolmaking—to the next generation. They taught by having young people help them do their work.

As ancient peoples gathered in cities, teaching became more of a profession. The educated made a living sharing their wisdom and knowledge with younger students. Imhotep, an ancient Egyptian architect, founded an architecture school. His students designed some of the earliest known Egyptian buildings. In ancient Greece, Plato and Socrates instructed Greek students in philosophy. One of Plato's students, Aristotle, tutored the future king, Alexander the Great. Ancient Rome had its teachers, as did Persia and India. Islamic leaders and scholars created universities from Baghdad, west to Spain, and south to Timbuktu in modern-day Mali.

In Christian Europe, the church and the monastery became the centers for learning. These schools catered

In the 1800s, many schools had just one room.
One teacher taught students of all ages.

mostly to noble families and monks. That would change
during the Renaissance. During that period, all people,
regardless of their social class, were encouraged to learn
certain knowledge considered important.

Clergymen dominated education in Europe and the United States into the 1800s. Others who taught tended to do so for a short time, until they started other careers that interested them.

As time passed, Americans and immigrants alike poured into cities. Education began to be seen as necessary for democracy. Education was also seen as a way to teach people from other countries how to be Americans. A public school system took shape. States and counties took over schools from religious groups and laid down standards. Teachers received special training and had to earn a license. Instead of everyone learning in one room, students were divided into grades. High schools and job training schools appeared. Textbooks were created to teach specific subjects such as math, geography, and English.

Men held most of the teaching jobs at the time. After the Civil War, however, more women began to teach.

Writers have a long history of starting their careers as teachers. Author Henry David Thoreau taught grade school in his mid-20s. He even opened his own school with his brother. Later, Thoreau wrote the American classic *Walden*. Louisa May Alcott, Thoreau's friend and student, worked as a teacher years before she wrote the novel *Little Women*. Willa Cather, one of the most important female American writers, spent six years as a teacher in a one-room schoolhouse. She later won the Pulitzer Prize for her book *One of Ours*. Charlotte Brönte taught in her native England and in Belgium. Her 1847 novel *Jane Eyre* was a huge success and continues to inspire readers and moviemakers.

The tradition continues today. Best-selling author Stephen King taught high school English in Maine while working on novels and short stories in his spare time. Why do you think so many writers start their careers as teachers?

In fact, it was one of the few occupations open to women. By 1900, females dominated the education field. But it was a tough job. Teachers endured poor pay and lack of respect. In addition, superiors expected them to obey a long list of rules. Teachers had to be cheerful, not complain, not get married, not wear makeup, and have a plain hairdo.

In the late 1950s, not only had men returned to teaching, but there were more men than women working at this job. But the numbers slowly changed back. As time passed, more women went to college and started careers. By 2003, about 75 percent of all public school teachers were women. In elementary schools, the percentage of teachers who are women is even higher.

Politicians continue to make education an important issue. Voters often list education as one of their top concerns. As America and the world become increasingly high-tech, learning to think and work with information becomes even more important. Good teachers are essential to giving students the tools they need to succeed.

CHAPTER TWO

ON THE JOB

After school, some teachers may be asked to make sure students get on the correct bus.

A teacher's day starts early. Often he or she arrives a half hour to an hour before the students. Many use the time to prepare the classroom, grade a few papers, check e-mail, and write progress reports for their students. On some mornings, a teacher may monitor the playground or direct students out of bus and car drop-off areas.

Teachers have to start the day energized. Why? Because students are sleepy as the school day begins. An elementary school teacher may kick off the day with a fun or unusual activity. High school teachers prefer to get right down to business. That's because there is a lot of information to cover in a short period of time.

Throughout the day, a teacher interacts with many different personalities. An elementary school teacher might have a room of 20 to 30 students. High school teachers get a new roomful every period. That can equal more than 100 faces each day. Each student learns and behaves in slightly different ways.

It's not easy to keep so many unique individuals interested or to take care of each of their needs. Sometimes teachers must deal with students who are noisy or disrespectful. Teachers help these students obey the classroom rules by talking with them. If this is not

*Staying organized
helps a teacher keep up
with paperwork.*

enough, the teacher may send students to the principal's office. They may also ask the student's parents to come to school to talk about how to get the student back on track.

During time outside the classroom, a teacher performs other necessary duties. In many schools, for example, teachers take turns monitoring the cafeteria at lunchtime, watching students at recess, and helping out in the library.

Teachers also get a period of work time away from students called the professional period. The professional period gives teachers a chance to grade papers and write reports. But teachers say it's not nearly enough time to finish their work. In fact, many have to use the period to catch up on other tasks or clean up their rooms. Sometimes the professional period is used to conduct a teachers' meeting.

For these and other reasons, a teacher's workday continues after the final bell. They are not paid for these extra hours. Schoolteachers often take home a large pile of papers to grade. The amount of added work depends on factors such as class size, where one teaches, and how long a teacher has been teaching. New, less-experienced teachers often have a hard time keeping up with the work at first.

Other duties after hours may include guiding children onto school buses, holding parent-teacher conferences, and talking to parents on the phone. Teachers may also be required to chaperone school events and dances and

Many teachers take part in extracurricular activities. These activities can range from leading the school choir to overseeing the school newspaper or coaching athletic teams. Teachers who take on these extra responsibilities must be comfortable using their skills in settings other than a formal classroom.

Some schools require teachers to take part in extracurricular activities. Others leave it up to the individual. The extracurricular activity a teacher chooses is sometimes, though not always, related to his teaching specialty. For instance, physical education teachers often coach sports. Music teachers may lead the chorus or rehearse actors for the school play.

Extracurricular activities offer teachers a chance to interact with students in different ways and pass along different skills. Many teachers report it to be one of the best parts of the job.

represent the school at special events in the community.

Teachers may also need to write their lesson plans at home in the evenings or on the weekend. A lesson plan sets the goals for what students will learn and helps the teacher to organize information. A good lesson plan covers the necessary information but is also flexible. That means a teacher can change it as the day goes along. Teachers use their own experience, material provided by the school district, books, and the Internet to draw up the plans. Lesson plans include tests or

The best teachers enjoy helping people learn.

student assignments. These show the teacher whether or not students have learned the material being taught.

Teachers sacrifice a lot of personal time to make sure that their lessons are planned well. They also make sure that they are doing everything they can to help their students succeed.

CHAPTER THREE

From Student to Teacher

Be confident and energetic when giving class presentations. This helps build the speaking skills you will need as a teacher.

One of the best ways to get a head start on a teaching career is to take classes that prepare you for college. Teaching today requires a college degree. The better prepared you are when you leave high school, the better your chances are to excel in college.

First, sign up for classes in the subjects

that interest you. Think you might want to teach history? Then learn as much history as you can, starting in high school. Interested in coaching track someday? Join the team. Do as much as you can. Ask questions. One of the great things about teaching is that it lets you use your own experiences to help others.

Communication is another big part of getting ready for a teaching career. As a teacher, you have to stand in a classroom and keep everyone's attention. A public speaking course, or even the drama club, teaches you how to be comfortable in front of people. English classes help you improve your writing, which is another key communication skill for teachers.

Summer breaks and time after school offer chances to get experience. Volunteering is an excellent start. Summer camps, community centers, day care facilities, and other organizations encourage students to apply for jobs working with young people. Many positions offer pay. And there's an added benefit. Working in these kinds of jobs shows a desire to teach. Having such experiences improves your chances of getting into a good college.

Once in college, you should take courses that provide a solid background in subjects such as science, math, history, and current events. The other courses you need depend on the subject you wish to teach. The age group you want to instruct matters, too. An elementary school teacher needs to know more than the facts of the subject she teaches. It's also important for her to understand how children think and develop, how to get them excited about a topic, and how to make a lesson plan.

No one expects incoming college students to know what subjects and grade levels they want to teach. But the sooner you make those decisions, the easier it is to decide on the right classes.

Teaching at a university requires at least a master's degree.

Teachers must know their subject matter. They also need to understand how students learn.

For secondary school teaching, you need even more knowledge of the subject. Secondary school teachers also need to understand how older students learn. These teachers spend more time giving and grading tests.

As your courses end, the on-the-job training begins. Colleges send their would-be teachers into schools as student teachers. A student teacher practices skills in the real world of the classroom while partnered with an experienced teacher. This lasts for about six months. Sometimes they student teach in schools attached to their college. Other times they student teach in public schools or sometimes in private schools.

Once you graduate from college, you start to look for a

Learning & Innovation Skills

Everyone hears the phrase "going to college," but what does it mean? It is important to understand your options so you choose the best educational path for you. Many students go to a four-year university with an education program. Others attend a teacher training college. These schools generally offer courses in specific subjects and education. A few specialize in certain kinds of teaching, such as Montessori education.

It's also possible to start at a community (or junior) college. This provides the first two years toward a college degree but costs far less than a four-year university. Some would-be teachers earn a four-year degree in a specific subject and then study teaching in order to teach their specialty. They return to college for an advanced degree, called a master's degree, and take the courses necessary to become a teacher.

job. Keep in mind that a teacher must earn a license, or certificate, from the state. In certain places, a teacher needs a license from the city where he or she wants to work. The requirements for a license include having a college degree and passing a special test. While job-hunting, you can scan newspapers, magazines, and Internet sites to see which schools need new teachers. Many universities and colleges also have a department, called the placement office, to help graduates find jobs.

THE FUTURE OF TEACHING

Today, many companies are doing business internationally. Employers sometimes hire teachers to teach workers the basics of a foreign language.

Jobs in teaching are expected to grow steadily in future years. The U.S. Department of Labor rates the new job opportunities as good to excellent. But the number of available jobs depends on many factors.

States with growing populations, such as many in the West or South, will see the largest increase in jobs. How

The teaching profession offers a variety of jobs outside of elementary and secondary schools. For example, some people prefer to tutor students after school. This can be preparing students for tests, giving music lessons, or many other things. Some classroom teachers even tutor as a second job to earn extra money.

Some companies also hire professional teachers to instruct their employees in new job skills, public speaking, or other areas. Teachers thrive in these positions because they are already experienced in getting others to learn. There are even teachers who teach other teachers. Experts believe opportunities for jobs outside the classroom will continue to grow.

we teach children also determines new job growth. For example, many places have increased programs for preschool and kindergarten. Certification in one of those specialties sometimes improves a person's chances of getting hired.

Jobs also tend to be easier to find in rural and inner-city areas. Both kinds of schools often pay less than others, have fewer supplies and facilities, and suffer from serious social problems. Because of that, some teachers prefer to look for jobs elsewhere.

Teachers of the future, like all of us, will have to deal with change. One of the big changes in education concerns technology. Teachers of today already use more than a chalkboard and books. They teach with computer technology such as the Internet and interactive whiteboards. They use audio and visual equipment such as DVD players.

Changes in society also influence how teachers do their jobs. In large cities, for instance, teachers today may have more immigrant students from foreign countries than in the recent past. This sometimes requires a teacher to be fluent in a second language. A teacher must also be familiar with the cultures that immigrant students come from. While many immigrants to the United States come from Spanish-speaking countries, teachers in Seattle and San Francisco also see children who were born in China. Those in Chicago sometimes teach Polish or Russian children in their classes.

Teachers today deal more with social problems than in the past. Many schools, especially high schools, offer

21st Century Content

In 2005–2006, public school teacher salaries averaged $49,026 per year. Salaries in California and Connecticut were the highest. Overall, secondary school teachers make slightly more than elementary school teachers. In many places, teachers with a master's degree earn higher pay.

Many leaders argue that communities need to offer better pay for teachers in order to attract the best candidates and retain the best teachers. But many residents don't want to pay the higher taxes that would be required to pay teachers more. What do you think? Should teachers be paid more? Would you be willing to pay higher taxes so that teachers could earn higher salaries?

classes in subjects such as drug education and suicide prevention. In addition, teachers are asked to watch for signs of troubled students, bullying, child abuse, and other problems. These responsibilities can add to a teacher's workload and stress.

In future years, teaching is sure to change. We'll have new technology and new ways of learning. We will always need good teachers. Teaching promises to remain a dynamic and rewarding profession well into the 21st century and beyond.

28

SOME FAMOUS TEACHERS

Charlotte Brönte (1816–1855) had her first teaching job at age 19 in Great Britain and later taught in Belgium. She is the author of *Jane Eyre*.

Willa Cather (1873–1947) taught high school English for six years while developing her creative writing skills. Her novel *My Ántonia* made her famous, and she later won the Pulitzer Prize.

Galileo Galilei (1564–1642) was a giant of the Renaissance. He tutored young Italian nobles in order to finance his scientific experiments.

Lyndon B. Johnson (1908–1973) was the 36th president of the United States. Earlier, he taught fifth- through seventh-grade students in Cotulla, Texas, and later was a speech teacher in Houston.

Stephen King (1947–) worked as an English teacher in Hampden, Maine, before becoming a best-selling novelist.

Sting (Gordon Sumner) (1951–) taught for two years prior to his career as a rock star.

Anne Sullivan (1866–1936) started tutoring six-year-old Helen Keller in 1887 and became her longtime teacher, supporter, and friend.

Laura Ingalls Wilder (1867–1957) is the author of the *Little House on the Prairie* books. She graduated from a teaching college at age 15 and took her first job in rural South Dakota.

Glossary

chaperone (SHAP-uh-rohn) to watch over social events such as dances

democracy (dih-MAH-kruh-see) a system of government in which the people choose their leaders in elections

dynamic (dye-NAM-ik) something that is energetic and constantly changing and growing

extracurricular (ek-struh-kuh-RIK-yuh-luhr) school activities outside the normal part of the day, such as sports, drama, or music

fluent (FLOO-uhnt) able to speak a language easily, or to know something very well

immigrants (IM-uh-gruhnts) people who come to a new country with the intention of staying there for good

lesson plans (LESS-uhn PLANZ) organized writings of what teachers intend to teach on each day

license (LYE-suhnss) a legal document that allows a person to teach in a specific state

monastery (MON-uh-ster-ee) a building, or number of buildings, used by people who have taken special religious vows

professional period (pruh-FESH-uh-nuhl PIHR-ee-uhd) time during the day when a teacher can work on grading papers, writing reports, or doing other tasks

Renaissance (REN-uh-sahnss) a period in European history from the late 1300s through the 1600s known for breakthroughs in science and the arts

student teachers (STOO-duhnt TEECH-uhrz) college students or recent college graduates working in real classrooms to get experience

tutored (TOO-turd) taught a lesson to one student

FOR MORE INFORMATION

Books

Loeb, Jason. *Global Perspectives: Education*. Ann Arbor, MI: Cherry Lake Publishing, 2008.

Parks, Peggy J. *Exploring Careers: Teacher*. Farmington Hills, MI: KidHaven Press, 2003.

Web Sites

Teach California
www.teachcalifornia.org/
Discover what it takes to be a teacher in California

U.S. Department of Labor: Teacher
www.bls.gov/k12/help01.htm
Learn more about what teachers do day-to-day

INDEX

Alcott, Louisa May, 10
Alexander the Great, 7
Aristotle (Greek
    philosopher), 7

behavior problems, 13–14,
    27–28
Brönte, Charlotte, 10

Cather, Willa, 10
cities, 7, 9, 27
certification, 26
clergymen, 8
communication, 19

democracy, 9
duties, 12, 13, 14, 15–17

education, 18–19, 20–22, 23
elementary schools, 10,
    13, 20, 28
energy, 13
extracurricular activities, 16

grade levels, 9, 21
grading, 12, 14, 15

high schools. See
    secondary schools.

homework, 15, 16

Imhotep (Egyptian
    architect), 7
immigrants, 9, 27
Internet, 16, 24, 27

job-hunting, 24
job opportunities, 25–26

kindergarten, 26
King, Stephen, 10

languages, 27
lesson plans, 16–17, 20
licensing, 9, 23–24

master's degrees, 23, 28
meetings, 14, 15
men, 10
monasteries, 7

on-the-job training, 22–23

parents, 14, 15
placement offices, 24
Plato (Greek philosopher), 7
politics, 11
prehistoric societies, 6

prep time, 12
preschools, 26
private schools, 23
professional period, 14–15
public schools, 9, 10, 23, 28

Renaissance, 7–8
rules, 10, 13

salaries, 9, 15, 19, 26, 28
secondary schools, 9, 10,
    13, 18, 19, 22, 27–28
social problems, 27–28
Socrates (Greek
    philosopher), 7
standards, 9
student teachers, 23

teacher training colleges,
    23
technology, 26–27
textbooks, 9
Thoreau, Henry David, 10
tutoring, 26

volunteering, 19–20

women, 9–10
work experience, 19–20

ABOUT THE AUTHOR

Kevin Cunningham is the author of 30 books, including
a series on diseases in history and a number of books in
Cherry Lake's Global Products series. He lives near Chicago,
Illinois.